CONTENTS

Beaver Scout Promise — 6

Beaver Scout Strip Story – Helping on the Farm — 7

Beaver Scout Board Game – Old Macdonald's Farm — 12

Digimon Strip Story – Having a Party! — 14

The C2K Challenge — 20

Secret Messages — 22

Story – Merlin Magpie — 24

Activity – Word Search — 26

Feature – Feathered Friends — 27

Activity – Spot the Changes — 30

Beaver Scouts' New Uniforms and the New Scout Logo — 32

Weirdest and Wackiest World Records — 34

Just Joking — 36

Beaver Scout's Local Stories — 38

Digimon Strip Story – Come the Flymon! — 40

Activity – Planets — 46

Competition – London Planetarium — 48

Beaver Scout Strip Story – Pocket Money — 56

BEAVER

SCOUT ANNUAL 2002

scouts
be prepared . . .

Pedigree®

Published by Pedigree Books Limited
The Old Rectory, Matford Lane, Exeter EX2 4PS
E-mail books@pedigreegroup.co.uk
Published in 2001

£5.99

The Beaver Scout Promise
I promise to do my best
To be kind and helpful
And to love God.

The Beaver Scout Motto
FUN AND FRIENDS

The Beaver Scout Badges
There are two Beaver Scout badges issued by the Beaver Scout Leader after periods of six to eight months.

To receive your first Beaver Scout Badge, you must take part with your Colony in an active and balanced Colony programme for six to eight months.

To receive the second Beaver Scout Badge, continue to take part in an active and balanced Colony programme for another further six to eight months.

HELPING ON THE FARM

10

OLD MACDONALD'S FARM

To play this game with a friend, you will need different coloured counters and a dice. Take turns to roll the dice and move that number of spaces around the board. If you land on a message, do whatever it tells you. The first to Old Macdonald's farmhouse, wins!

START

1 2 3 4 5 6 7

27 28 29 30 31 32 33 34 35 36 37

Beware of the bull. Go back to START!

38 Chickens chase you on to FINISH

39 40 41 42 43 44

15

16

THE C2K CHALLENGE

33 Colonies of Beaver Scouts in the UK completed the Scouting Magazine Millennium Challenge last year. The aim of the challenge was to score a minimum of 2,000 points during the year 2000, by completing various tasks based on the Beaver Scout Challenge Badge.

In order to score points, each Colony had to complete at least one task in each of these four Challenge areas:

- **Caring Challenge**
- **Exploring Challenge**
- **Scouting Challenge**
- **Personal Challenge**

CARING CHALLENGE

These Beaver Scouts from the 28th Willesden Colony donated blankets to their local RSPCA shelter. Just purrrrfect for cold nights!

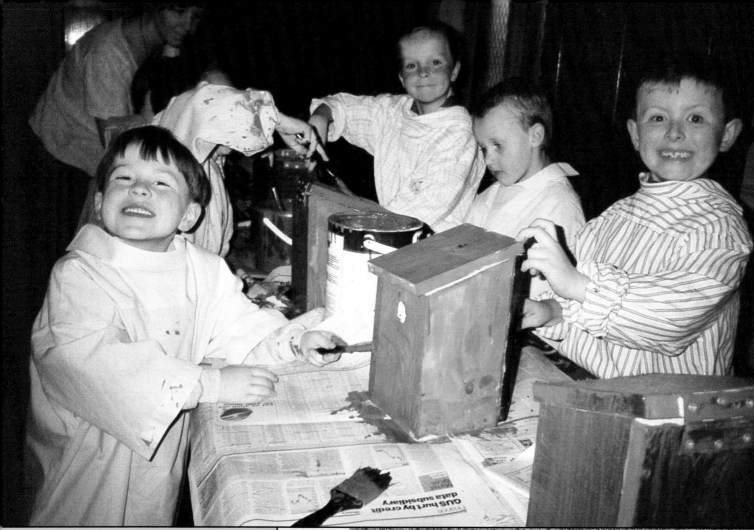

PERSONAL CHALLENGE

The 11th Blackpool Colony made these brilliant bird boxes which they took home for their gardens. They even completed surveys of all the birds they attracted. These Beaver Scouts are certainly no bird-brains!

EXPLORING CHALLENGE

Beaver Scouts from the 28th Lincoln Colony did a riverbank walk. Then, when the Lincoln town crier visited their colony, they got to try on his hat and coat – and even ring his bell. Oy-ye! Oy-ye! The Beaver Scout belled – I mean 'yelled'!

ACTIVITY

SECRET MESSAGES

So you want to send a message to a friend – but you don't want anyone else to be able to read it... not even your nosy little brother? Well, here are a few different ways for you to write a secret message, but don't tell anyone else, will you!

CANDLE WRITING

1 Use the candle as if it was a marker to write your secret message. Remember to press quite firmly.

You will need:

plain paper
candle
coloured ink
paint brush

2 Only when ink is lightly brushed over the paper will your message be revealed. Make sure you tell your friends how to 'read' the message when it arrives, otherwise they'll think you've sent them a sheet of blank paper!

LEMON LETTERS

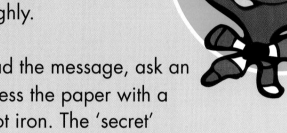

1 Use the toothpick dipped in lemon juice to write your message on a sheet of plain paper. Then let the juice dry thoroughly.

You will need:

an adult's help
lemon juice
toothpick
iron
plain paper

2 To read the message, ask an adult to press the paper with a medium-hot iron. The 'secret' message should soon be visible.

FEELING BLUE

1 In the saucepan, mix the cornstarch and water together

2 Ask an adult to help you cook the mixture for two minutes, stirring several times

You will need:

an adult's help
1 teaspoon
(5 g) cornstarch
60ml water
small saucepan
wooden spoon
iodine
sponge
plain paper

3 Leave to cool, then use the liquid to write your message on plain paper

4 When dry, lightly sponge the paper with a solution of iodine and water (10 drops in 60ml of water). Your writing will appear in dark blue and the paper will be light blue.

MERLIN MAGPIE

Baz and Daz were playing in the garden when Sarah arrived.

"Do you want to see the necklace and bracelet I made using milk bottle tops?" asked Sarah.

"Yes, but come and look at all the different badges we've collected first," said Baz.

Sarah dropped her necklace and bracelet on the garden table and followed Baz and Daz.

"I've brought my badges, too," said Sarah, emptying her little bag onto a bench. "I'll swap you that shiny red badge for a Liverpool football badge – I've got two of those!"

"I'll swap one of my Manchester United badges for that square badge," said Daz.

When they had finished swapping badges, Baz said, "Come on, Sarah. Let's look at your jewellery."

Sarah led the two boys over to the table where she had left her necklace and bracelet.

"They're not here!" said Sarah. "I know I left them on this table."

"Don't be silly, they can't have just disappeared," said Daz, bending down to look under the table.

The friends searched everywhere, but Sarah's jewellery definitely had disappeared!
"Oh, come on. Let's look at our badges again," said Sarah, at last.

But when they went back to the bench, Daz gasped, "My favourite orange badge has gone!"
"I haven't got it," said Sarah.
"Me, neither," said Baz. "There's something very strange going on here!"

Just then, the three friends heard a rustling sound. Looking up into the branches of a tree, they saw a magpie returning to its nest – and it was holding Sarah's bracelet in its beak!
"So that's where our things have disappeared to!" laughed Baz.

"That magpie has taken them to put in its nest!" said Sarah.
"Magpie's like collecting shiny objects."
Later, when the magpie had flown away, Baz's dad climbed a ladder and found the missing badge, the necklace and the bracelet.
"We should call that bird Merlin Magpie, because it makes things disappear – just like magic!" laughed Daz.

WORDSEARCH

The birds listed below appear on this grid up, down across
and diagonally. As you find each name, draw a circle around it.
The letters left over spell another kind of bird that lays huge eggs -
and is unable to fly. Do you know what it is?

MAGPIE

TERN

SWAN

WREN

STARLING

O	G		N	O	N	S
E	N	E	R	W	O	S
H	I	T	E	L	E	E
S	L	P	T		G	A
U	R	R	G	N	I	G
R	A	I	A	A	P	U
H	T	W	C	H	M	L
T	S	D	U	C	K	L

OWL

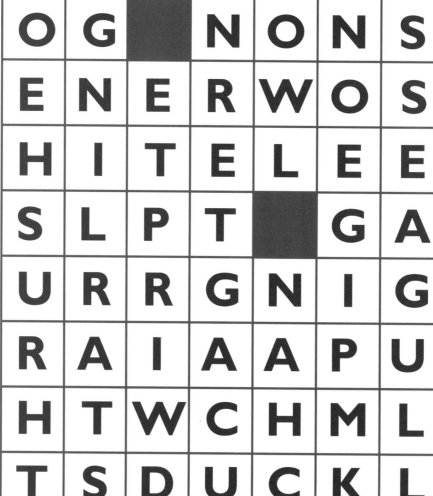

DUCK

THRUSH

PIGEON

SEAGULL

FEATHERED FRIENDS!

With winter here, Beaver Scouts could do a good deed for birds by making sure they have enough to eat. With the cold, damp British weather (YUUUCCK!), Birds need regular supplies food if they are going to survive.

With the ground becoming hard, it makes it difficult for birds to reach the bugs, beetles and worms on which they feed. With food so difficult to come by, many birds do not live through the harsh winter conditions.

To help them, you could encourage birds to visit your garden to feed. Not only will you be doing them a big favour, once they understand that there is a regular supply of food to be had, they will continue to visit your garden even during the warmer months.

Feeding birds doesn't take a lot of time or effort, and you'll be rewarded by the sight of many different birds visiting your garden. If you don't have a garden, you can always put out scraps on your windowsill, or ask your Pack Leader's permission to set up a bird-feeding area outside your Pack's meeting place!

To set up a 'feeding area', use a simple tray, either placed at ground level (for ground-feeding birds) or hung by wire from the branch of a tree. Remember, cats will attack birds, so place the tray where they can't reach it!

Many people have a bird table in their garden. (Perhaps your Pack Leader could help you build one?) The bird table needs to be placed somewhere to protect the birds from both the heat of the sun and strong winds. Add a roof to save birds getting soaked when it rains! To encourage different types of birds to visit your table, decorate it with peanut holders, tit-bells, seed hoppers and hanging baskets.

Change food daily, otherwise it will go mouldy, and the table should be cleaned at least once a week. (If you leave gaps in each corner of the table's frame, it will make the job of brushing away unwanted food that much easier!)

27

What should you feed them? Well, like us, birds are happy to eat almost anything! Many birds love peanuts (not the salted type!), and seeds such as corn, millet and maize are appreciated, too. Potato, bread and cake crumbs, dry oats, biscuit crumbs, fresh coconut and home-made bird-cake are all foods that will have a colourful variety of birds swooping down to your bird table!

Also, fruits and berries, animal fats such as bacon rinds, tinned pet food, mealworms and maggots go down a treat!

Birds need regular supplies of water, for both drinking and bathing, especially in winter, as it not only refreshes but helps them to keep their feathers clean. A simple saucer of water will do, but it must be changed daily. This also allows you to check that the water hasn't become frozen!

Why not keep a diary of how many different types of birds come to feed from your table?. You could note down the date, time and weather conditions when you first see a new species. And include drawings or photographs to make your diary more interesting!

FOR MORE INFORMATION ON BIRDS, CONTACT THE

Royal Society for the Protection of Birds
(RSPB)
UK Headquarters
The Lodge
Sandy
Bedfordshire   SG19 2DL

Ask for details to become a member of the Young Ornithologists' Club. Please do remember to enclose a large A4 stamped addressed envelope when you write!

MAKING A BIRD-CAKE

If you want to help the birds this winter, why not make a delicious bird-cake for them to feed on?

YOU WILL NEED:

INGREDIENTS:
fat or lard, chopped nuts, cake-crumbs or bread-crumbs, and oatmeal.

UTENSILS:
A mixing bowl, large plastic drinking cup, spoon, scissors and a long piece of string.

1 Soften the fat or lard in a saucepan (ask an adult or your Colony Leader to help you). Add the melted fat to the mix of nuts, oatmeal and crumbs in a bowl and mix together.

2 Cut a long piece of string. Tie a really big knot in one end and put the string into the cup so that the knotted end is at the bottom. Then spoon the mixture into the cup.

3 Wait until the mixture is set and cold and then gently pull on the string to remove the cake from the cup.

4 Tie your bird-cake from a tree branch or windowsill and wait for the birds to come swooping down to feed!

WARNING Scissors are sharp and dangerous. Ask a grown-up to do the cutting for you, or make sure one is nearby when you do it yourself.

SPOT THE CHANGES

We took two pictures of this group of Beaver Scouts crossing a rope bridge, but, it seems that our camera has decided to play a trick on us and has made some changes to one snapshot. Can you Spot all 6 changes?

Answers: Blue T-shirt became orange, Beaver Scout missing from background, rope bridge section missing, first Beaver Scout on rope bridge has a badge missing on his hat, middle Beaver Scout on rope bridge sock has become shorter, last Beaver Scout on rope bridge has scarf missing.

NEW UNIFORMS AND SCOUT LOGO

It has been almost 34 years since The Scout Association last made any major changes to its identity - long, long before you were even born!

But for the new millennium we've come up with some great new ideas, which we think you'll all like! Included in our changes are brand new uniforms for Scouts, as well as new Scout logo that reflects the Movement's history, while bringing us up to date.

scouts
be prepared . . .

The new uniforms for the UK's half a million Scouts were revealed back in February, on the 144th anniversary of Baden-Powell's birth. Over the next two years, these uniforms will be gradually introduced, until January 2003, when you'll all be wearing them!

Back in February 2001, six children from the Scout Movement appeared on BBC's Blue Peter programme to show-off the brand new uniforms. Laura, Andre, Sam, Ellen, Katie and Robert did a great job of modelling the outfits, - and were even joined by Meg, Blue Peter's new puppy!

Out goes the old mushroom brown and grey colour and in comes turquoise, teal green, navy blue, beige and stone.

For all you Beaver Scouts, there's a great new turquoise sweatshirt and Group scarf. And if the sun keeps shining, you can wear the new turquoise short-sleeved polo shirt and baseball cap!

All your clothing will have the new Scout logo, too!

WEIRDEST, WACKIEST, RECORD BREAKERS

SUPER SPAGHETTI SUCKER

An Englishman managed to get into the record books by ploughing his way through a staggering 100 yards of spaghetti in 12.02 seconds! Do you think he ordered it all from the same takeaway?

SHEEP SHEARERS SHEER SHEEP

In Western Australia, one man sheared a record number of 390 lambs in just 8 hours. Talk about a close shave!

BIGGEST BUBBLE-GUM BUBBLE

The biggest reported diameter of a bubble-gum bubble is 58.4 cm (23 in). Trouble is, there's only one way to make a bubble disappear!

FEET FIRST

A boy, who stands 2.29 m (7 ft 6 in) tall, has the largest feet ever recorded. Can you believe he wears size 28 shoes! Still, at least he can always let a friend stay the night – and make a bed up for him inside one of his furry slippers!

STICKY SITUATION

Strange, but true! It's actually been recorded that someone in the UK has collected around 3,750 unused sticking plasters of all different colours, styles, shapes and sizes. Why, you might ask? We haven't got a clue!

PASS THE DEODORANT

A South American birds called a hoatzin gives off an odour very similar to cow manure. The reason for its awful smell is probably due to a combination of its diet of green leaves and unusual digestive system.

CHEMICALLY COMPLEX CHOCOLATE

Chocolate, which was invented 2,000 years ago, contains around 300 chemicals, including caffeine. Now are you still going to eat it? Of course you are!

FASTEST BED RACERS

The fastest bed race took part in the UK, when a bed was pushed 3.27 km (2 miles 56 yards) in 12 minutes 9 seconds!

TIDDLYWINKS JUMP

The highest recorded tiddlywinks jump stands at 3.49 metres (11 ft 5 in).

CHERRY STONE SPIT

The longest recorded distance that a cherry stone has been spat is 28.98 metres (95 ft 1 in). I hope he picked up the stone afterwards!

JUST JOKING!

Q: Who invented fractions ?
A: Henry the 1/8!

Q: What does 'Minimum' mean?
A: A very small mother!

Q: How do you catch a
runaway dog?
A: Hide behind a tree and make a
noise like a bone!

Q: What did
the idiot call his pet zebra?
A: Spot !

Q: What do
you call medicine for horses?
A: Cough stirrup!

Q: Why did the
boy hold his shoe to his ear?
A: Because he liked
sole music!

Q: Where do you
find a birthday present for a cat?
A: In a cat-alogue!

Q: What party
game do rabbits like to play?
A: Musical Hares.

Q: Where do
astronauts leave their spaceships?
A: At parking meteors !

THE REAL MEANING OF WORDS!

ABUNDANCE
Lots of dancing cakes

APRICOTS
Beds for baby monkeys

AUTOGRAPH
A chart showing the sales of cars

WAITER
Someone who thinks money grows on trays

WATCHDOG
An animal that goes 'woof, tick, woof, tick, woof, tick'

OCTOPUS
A cat with eight feet

TONGUE TWISTER
Something that gets your tang tongueled

EARWIG
A piece of false hair worn over the ears

ELASTIC BAND
Group who play rubber instruments

ELECTRIC EEL
Fish that swims in strong currents

MORE LOCAL BEAVER SCOUT STORIES

Last year, the 30th S.W. Cheshire (Hightown) Beaver Scout Group took up Scouting Magazine's challenge – and made a banner out of 2000 pieces of material to celebrate the millennium. They used foam, paper, felt – and any other materials they could find!

The Beaver Scouts and Cub Scouts of the 1st Trowell (St Helen's) Scout Group rallied together and gave all their outgrown videos to the children's ward of Queens Medical Centre in Nottinghamshire.

Luke Walker from the Penzance/Newlyn Scout Colony made his promise to the Beaver Colony at the first and last signpost in England. Have any other Beavers made their promise in any unusual places?

Despite the rain, Beaver Scouts from all over Humberside flocked to last year's Humberside Beaver Scout fun day, where face painting was a big hit!

When Baden-Powel visited Africa in 1888, he met a Zulu Chief - Chief Dinizulu. From this meeting, the Scout Movement inherited the left handshake - a sign of friendship. The 49th (St Peter's) Beaver Scout Colony were amazed to discover that Jack Ricketts, the great-great-grandson of Chief Dinizulu, was going to be a new Member of their Group!

41

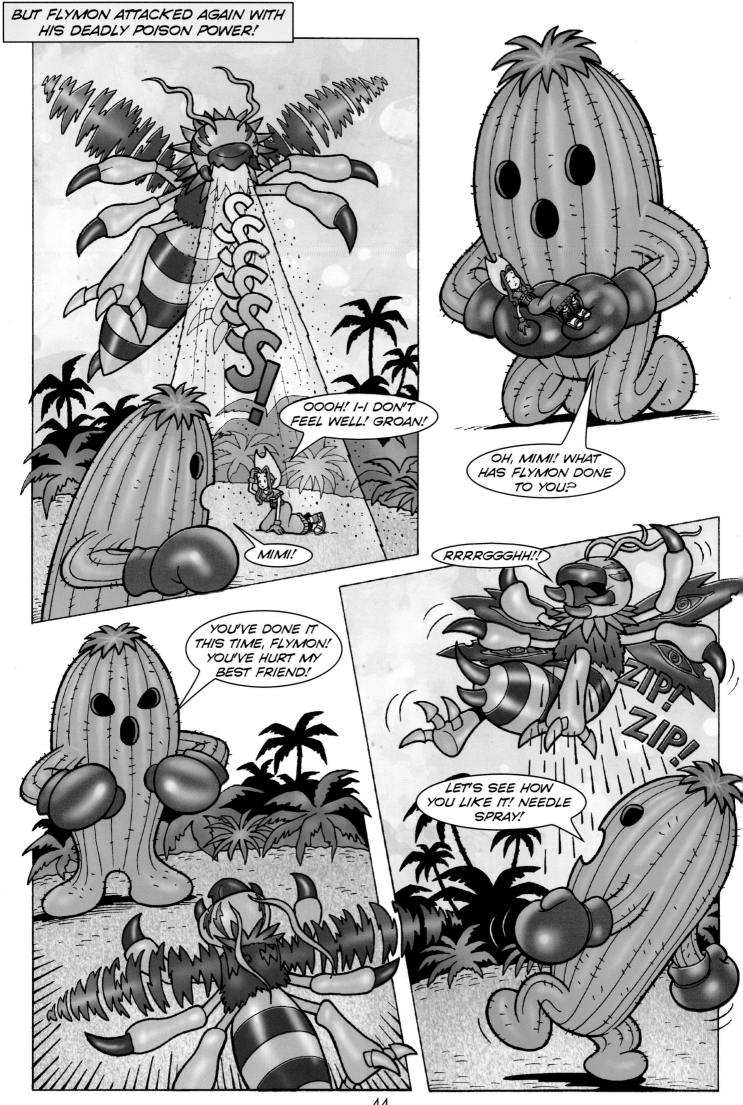

PLANETS

Did you know that there are nine planets in our solar system! Rearrange the letters beside each planet to spell its name. Then you can read some interesting facts about each one.

CRUMERY

Named after the Roman god of commerce and thievery because it moves quickly across the sky.

NEVUS

Named for the Roman mythological goddess of love and beauty because it is bright and easy to see.

HEART

This is the only planet that is not named for a Greek or Roman mythical character.

SARM

This planet is named after the god of war from Roman myth.

TIERPUJ

Named for the Roman king of the gods
(Zeus in Greek mythology).

TRANUS

Saturday is named
after this planet.

PEENNUT

Named after the Roman
mythological god of the sea.

TOPUL

Named for the mythological
Roman god of the underworld,
because it is dark and cold.

NUSAUR

Named for the Greek mythological
god of the heavens.

LONDON PLANETARIUM

We couldn't believe how many of you entered last year's Cub Scout and Beaver Scout Competitions, hoping to win a free Beaver Colony or Cub Pack visit to a Sea Life Centre. Details of last year's lucky Beaver Scout winner is on page 55. Now, as there's a Beaver Scout Annual AND a Cub Scout Annual this year, we're giving you Beaver Scouts the chance to enter your very own competition! So if you didn't win last year, try again! All you have to do is...

Answer the easy-peasy question...

Complete the entry form...

And pop it in the post!

WIN THIS FANTASTIC PRIZE!

A Beaver Colony visit to the London Planetarium and Madame Tussaud's (for up to 30 children and 6 accompanying adults)

With star-studded shows in the great green dome, the world famous London Planetarium has entertained millions of visitors for almost 40 years! You can have fun taking part in interactive demonstrations, find out what's the hottest spot in our Solar System – and learn all about the mysteries of space! If you're the lucky Beaver Scout winner of this year's competition, you and your Beaver Colony, plus six grown-ups, can make a combined visit to the London Planetarium and Madame Tussaud's absolutely free! Thanks to the generosity of Madame Tussaud's, you'll have a brilliant day out to remember forever!

TUSSAUD'S
LONDON
PLANETARIUM

Under the London Planetarium's huge dome, you can watch millions of twinkling stars as they emerge from a darkening sky. Learn all about the nine different planets in our Solar System – and what their names are. Find out what a black hole really is – and how artificial satellites give us information about our own planet.

You can find out more about Helen Sharman, Britain's first female astronaut, who set off to the Mir Space Station in 1991. ▶

Did you know that when you look into space you are looking backwards in time! For instance, light from the Andromeda Galaxy started 2 million years ago, making it the furthest object you can see with the naked eye!

Our planet Earth is really just a tiny speck in the universe - and it is just one of the nine planets orbiting the star we call the Sun. Many of these planets have their own orbiting satellites or moons which, with asteroids, meteors and even visiting comets, make up the Solar System.

▶ Of all the other planets, Mars – which is about 228 million km from the Sun, is the least hostile, and the most likely to be visited by humans one day.

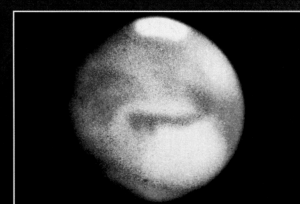

MADAME TUSSAUD'S LONDON

Madame Tussaud's has entertained and amazed people from all over the world for over 200 years! With a celebrity list of around 400 lifelike wax figures, it's difficult to know where to start first!

You can get a close-up look at some famous film stars like Pierce Brosnan and pop stars like Kylie Minogue!

See the world's top sporting stars, like Tim Henman.

▼ and even stop to have a chat with Barbara Windsor from Eastenders! But don't get too carried away. Remember, they're only wax models, after all!

If you're not lucky enough to win this year's competition and get your Beaver Colony to the London Planetarium and Madame Tussaud's absolutely free, discount tickets are available for groups on certain days. For more details contact the Customer Services Centre on: 0870 400 3010, or the London Planetarium web site at: http://www.london-planetarium.com

COMPETITION QUESTION

Which planet is the most likely to be visited by humans one day?

URANUS   MARS

JUPITER   PLUTO

SATURN   VENUS

NEPTUNE

MERCURY

If you think you know the correct answer, write it down on the entry form on the next page.

Then, in the space provided, say what you enjoy most about being a

Beaver Scout. Finally, fill in the information about yourself.

The completed entry form needs to be cut out and sent in. (If you don't want to spoil your annual, you can photocopy the form.) Send your entry to:

BEAVER SCOUT ANNUAL
2002 COMPETITION
THE SCOUT ASSOCIATION
GILWELL PARK
CHINGFORD
LONDON
E4 7QW

Please don't forget to put a stamp on your envelope. The Post Office will not deliver any unstamped entries.

CLOSING DATE FOR COMPETITION: FEBRUARY 28 2002

After this closing date, all the correct entries will be put in a big box and shaken. Then one form will be selected completely at random. The lucky winner will be informed by post and details published in the Beaver Scout Annual 2003.

BEAVER SCOUT ANNUAL 2002 COMPETITION

Which planet is the most likely to be visited by humans one day?

_____

What I enjoy most about being a Beaver Scout is (no more than 20 words):

_____

_____

_____

_____

My name is: _____   My age is: _____

My home address is: _____

Postcode: _____

My Beaver Colony is: _____

RULES OF ENTRY You do not need to have bought the Beaver Scout Annual to enter. Entries are limited to one per person. The decision of the Selection Panel is final. No person connected with the production of the Beaver Scout Annual 2002 is allowed to enter.

The prize is free entry to the London Planetarium and Madame Tussaud's for a Beaver Colony of up to 30 children and 6 adults. No cash alternative.

COMPETITION 2001

We had a fantastic response to last year's Cub Scout and Beaver Scout Annual 2001 competition. Thank you to everyone who wrote in. Although there could only be two winners, here are some of the answers we received when we asked...

What do you enjoy most about being a Beaver Scout?

I like Beavers because it makes me happy
and it's fun, fun, fun!
Thomas Williams, age 8

I like playing games. I like going on trips. I
enjoy making friends. I like collecting
Beaver badges.
Christopher Cartwright, age 7

I like wearing my uniform with badges and
playing games with my friends.
Sam Crawford, age 6

I like everything we do
Luke McCreary, age 6

I like playing the games that Bigwig
makes up.
Kearan Willis, age 6

I have just joined the Beavers and everyone
is kind to me. I play lots of fun games.
Adam Parke, age 6

I like Beavers because I make friends and
get to go on trips and get to sing at Eric
Morcambe's house.
Barry Matthews, age 7

Best of all Beavers is fun
Exciting games
And making things
Very good friends
Everyone
Remembers
Sharing and caring
Sam Bannister, age 7

I like playing games and having the badges
on me.
Luke Whittacker, age 8

I like to carry the flag on parade
I like Beaver parties
like playing 'Kingy!'
Edmund Hull, age 7

And finally... the Beaver Scout winner, who wrote...

I like everything about the Beavers, except the floor is cold!
Anthony Howith, age 7

EXTRA POCKET MONEY

"Look, there's a funfair opening today!" said Daz, pointing to a poster. "Let's ask Sarah if she want's to come with us." "Yippee! I love funfairs!" said Baz. "I like the Big Dipper and the Waltzer and the Ghost Train – as long as someone's with me, and..."

"Um, just one problem," said Daz, turning out his trouser pockets. "I don't have any money!" "Me, neither!" sighed Baz, pulling a sticky toffee out of his pocket. The two friends looked back at the poster and sighed.

"Come on, I'll empty my piggybank and treat you to a ride at the fair!" said Baz. "I might even have enough for a great big sticky toffee apple each! "Yippee again! cheered Daz as the two Beavers ran all the way home.

56

Running upstairs to his bedroom, Baz grabbed his piggybank and tipped it upside-down over the bed. "Oh, no! we won't get far with those!" gasped Daz, as a marble and two shirt buttons dropped out.

When Sarah arrived a little later, Baz and Daz told her about the fair. "We don't have any money to go, though," sighed Daz. "I know! Let's do some jobs and earn extra pocket money," smiled Sarah. "Then we can all go to the fair together".

"Dad said he'll give us some money for washing his car!" said Baz, coming out of his house with a bucket of soapy water and some cloths.

"This is harder than I thought it would be!" puffed Sarah, as she rubbed and scrubbed the car with one of the cloths. "And it's taking ages!" said Baz, coming out of his house with a bucket of soapy water and some cloths.

"Stand back, everyone. One... two... three... " said Daz, picking up the bucket of soapy water and aiming it at the car. Baz and Sarah could see what was about to happen, but didn't have time to tell Daz.

Instead of going over the car, the water goes all over Baz's dad, as he comes out of his house! "Um, I guess this means we won't be getting paid for cleaning your car, doesn't it? said Baz.

Getting Sarah's mum's shopping didn't earn the Beavers any extra money, either! "Oops!" gasped Daz, as the shopping handle snapped - and the shopping rolled down a hill. "Come back!" called Sarah, trying to catch the potatoes.

Taking the neighbour's dog for a walk was a disaster, too! "Hey, I'm supposed to be taking you for a walk!" cried Sarah, as the big hairy dog pulled her across the flower beds.

"Which one of you said 'let's take a dog for a walk'?" gasped Sarah, as the huge dog changed direction and ran past the two boys. The dog did eventually stop, but only after it had run round and round the garden, flattening almost every flower in sight!

At last, things seemed to be going well. The friends had managed to get a job weeding a garden. "Phew! I've never seen weeds this big before!" said Daz.

OH NOOOOO!

"Fancy pulling up all the plants!" gasped Sarah, as they walked home. "Awww, how was I to know they weren't weeds?" mumbled Daz. "They all look the same to me." "Now he tells us!" gasped Baz.

Suddenly, a light bulb seemed to flash inside Daz's head. "I know how we can earn some extra money!" he said making his two friends jump.

"If it's got anything to do with gardening, forget it!" said Baz. "Or getting shopping, or taking dogs for walks!" said Sarah. "No this is going to be easy- and lots of fun." smiled Daz.

At last, the Beaver Scouts thought of another way to raise some pocket money. They asked their parents if they could sell all their old, unwanted books and toys. Before long the Beaver Scouts had sold everything - and had collected a big jar of coins.

"Instead of going to the funfair, why don't we ask our Beaver Scout Leader if we can give the money we've raised to a charity?" said Sarah. Baz and Daz thought that was a great idea. WELL DONE, BEAVER SCOUTS!